6 e27

966.3
SEN

Senegal in pictures

015018

DATE	ISSUED TO	9.95

966.3
SEN

Senegal in pictures

015018

SENEGAL

...in Pictures

SENEGAL

...in Pictures

Prepared by
Geography Department

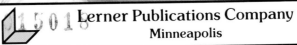 Lerner Publications Company
Minneapolis

Independent Picture Service

Senegalese fishermen gather their catch after a day at sea.

This is an all-new edition of the Visual Geography Series. Previous editions have been published by Sterling Publishing Company, New York City, and some of the original textual information has been retained. New photographs, maps, charts, captions, and updated information have been added. The text has been entirely reset in 10/12 Century Textbook.

LIBRARY OF CONGRESS CATALOGING-IN-PUBLICATION DATA

Senegal in pictures.

(Visual geography series)
Rev. ed. of: Senegal in pictures / prepared by Eugene Gordon.
Includes index.
Summary: Introduces the land, history, government, natural resources, culture, and people of the Republic of Senegal, situated on the westernmost bulge of the African continent.
1. Senegal. [1. Senegal] I. Gordon, Eugene, 1923- . Senegal in pictures. II. Lerner Publications Company. Geography Dept. III. Series: Visual geography series (Minneapolis, Minn.)
DT549.22.S46   1988   966.3   87-21347
ISBN 0-8225-1827-9 (lib. bdg.)

International Standard Book Number: 0-8225-1827-9
Library of Congress Catalog Card Number: 87-21347

VISUAL GEOGRAPHY SERIES®

Publisher
Harry Jonas Lerner
Associate Publisher
Nancy M. Campbell
Senior Editor
Mary M. Rodgers
Editor
Gretchen Bratvold
Illustrations Editor
Karen A. Sirvaitis
Consultants/Contributors
Thomas O'Toole
Sandra K. Davis
Designer
Jim Simondet
Cartographer
Carol F. Barrett
Indexer
Sylvia Timian
Production Manager
Richard J. Hannah

Independent Picture Service

A young woman from Kayar in western Senegal carries an enameled pan on her head.

Acknowledgments

Title page photo by Virginia M. Graham.

Elevation contours adapted from *The Times Atlas of the World,* seventh comprehensive edition (New York: Times Books, 1985).

1 2 3 4 5 6 7 8 9 10 97 96 95 94 93 92 91 90 89 88

These women are carrying bundles of *kinkeliba*, a tree from which a medicine is made that can reduce fever.

Contents

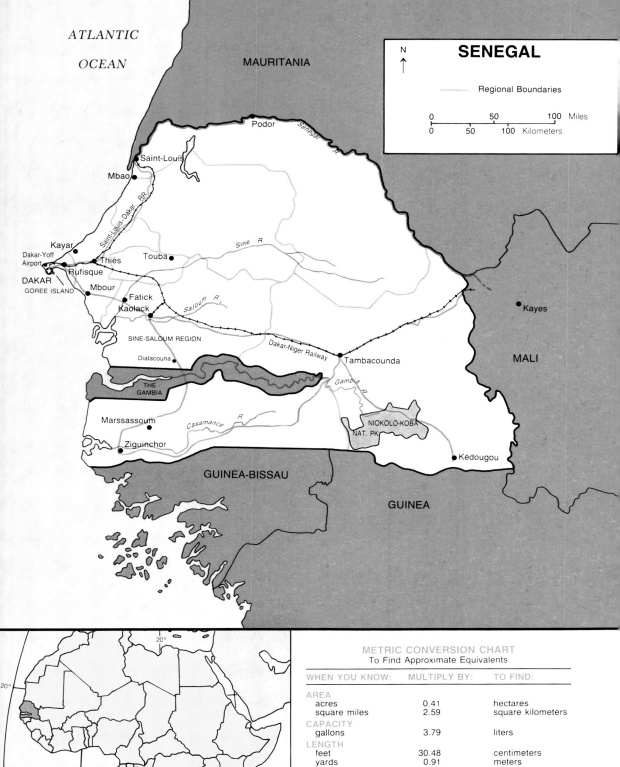

ATLANTIC

OCEAN

MAURITANIA

SENEGAL

N

Regional Boundaries

0   50   100 Miles
0   50   100 Kilometers

Podor

Senegal R.

Saint-Louis

Mbao

Saint-Louis–Dakar RR

Sine R.

Kayar

Dakar-Yoff
Airport

Thiès

Touba

Rufisque

DAKAR

Mbour

GOREE ISLAND

Fatick

Saloum R.

Kaolack

Kayes

MALI

SINE-SALOUM REGION

Dialacouna

Dakar-Niger Railway

Tambacounda

Gambia R.

THE
GAMBIA

Marssassoum

Casamance R.

NIOKOLO-KOBA
NAT. PK.

Ziguinchor

Kédougou

GUINEA-BISSAU

GUINEA

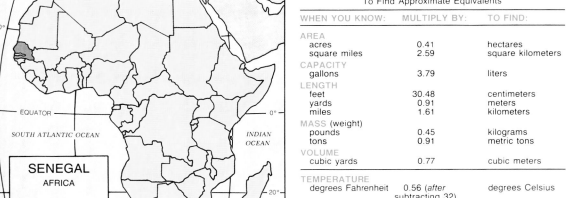

20°

20°

20°

EQUATOR

0°

SOUTH ATLANTIC OCEAN

INDIAN
OCEAN

20°

SENEGAL
AFRICA

0   1000 Miles
0   1000 Kilometers

METRIC CONVERSION CHART
To Find Approximate Equivalents

WHEN YOU KNOW:	MULTIPLY BY:	TO FIND:
AREA		
acres	0.41	hectares
square miles	2.59	square kilometers
CAPACITY		
gallons	3.79	liters
LENGTH		
feet	30.48	centimeters
yards	0.91	meters
miles	1.61	kilometers
MASS (weight)		
pounds	0.45	kilograms
tons	0.91	metric tons
VOLUME		
cubic yards	0.77	cubic meters
TEMPERATURE		
degrees Fahrenheit	0.56 (*after* subtracting 32)	degrees Celsius

The island of Gorée, just off the coast of Senegal, served as a slave-trading center in the seventeenth century.

Introduction

On the westernmost bulge of the African continent lies the Republic of Senegal, a small country with a rich history that reflects its varied peoples. Beginning in the tenth century, Senegal had regular trade and intellectual contact with the Islamic world. The first Europeans arrived in the middle of the fifteenth century, when Portuguese navigators reached the coast and established commercial bases.

After the discovery of the New World, European settlers required a cheap labor force to work on the agricultural plantations they established. These labor needs caused slavery to expand into an enormous financial enterprise. Most of the slaves were taken from the Guinea coast, an area that extended from Senegal eastward to the mouth of the Zaire (formerly the Congo) River. A few hundred years

7

A cattle farmer from northern Senegal pumps water for his animals. The effects of advancing desert lands, caused by deforestation and overgrazing, have made water for livestock more scarce in this region.

later, the French came to colonize most of West Africa, using Senegal as their administrative headquarters. Independence was achieved in 1960 under the leadership of the poet-statesman, Léopold Sédar Senghor.

Senegal has many faces. In the south, near the Guinean border, farmers cultivate small plots of land surrounded by wooded areas. In the west and north, Senegalese who raise livestock bring their cattle, sheep, and goats to and from seasonal pastures on the fringes of the Sahara Desert. Dakar, the capital, is one of Africa's most developed cities, with beautiful, broad avenues and modern office buildings, as well as middle-class dwellings and miserable slums.

Despite the influences of Europe, however, Senegal is still an African nation. The Wolof language predominates, and clothing styles and daily patterns of behavior are very much a part of the West African heritage to which Senegal has been closely tied throughout its history.

Women in Dakar wait on shore for the arrival of fishermen, with whom the women will bargain for the fresh haul of seafood.

Sandy beaches and small bays carve the coastline of the Cap-Vert Peninsula, where Dakar is located.

1) The Land

Senegal, situated on the western tip of Africa, covers an area of about 76,000 square miles—roughly the size of the state of Nebraska. Senegal is bordered on the north by Mauritania, on the east by Mali, on the south by Guinea and Guinea-Bissau, and on the west by the Atlantic Ocean. The long, narrow Republic of the Gambia penetrates Senegal for 200 miles beginning at the mouth of the Gambia River. The Gambian republic nearly cuts off the southern part of Senegal, called the Casamance. Since February 1, 1982, the two countries have been linked in the Senegambian Confederation.

Topography

Senegal consists mostly of low, rolling plains. In the southeast the land rises to an elevation of 1,640 feet to form the foothills of the Fouta Djallon Mountains, which are located across the border in Guinea. Despite Senegal's unvaried topography, five geographical regions—the coastal zone, the Senegal River Valley, the Ferlo, the eastern region, and the Casamance—have been identified.

The coastal zone extends for about 310 miles along the Atlantic Ocean and is characterized by sandy beaches and occasional sandbars. Roughly in the middle of the

9

coastal zone is the Cap-Vert Peninsula, which includes the capital city of Dakar. Toward the north, the coastal belt is about 15 to 20 miles wide and curves to form an estuary (a channel where the river meets the sea). The southern half of the zone is much narrower, with creeks, channels, and flat, swampy islands overgrown with mangrove thickets.

A parched land that receives little rainfall, the Senegal River Valley is nourished by the annual flooding of the Senegal River. Most of the valley is 10 miles wide, but it broadens to a width of about 35 miles before it reaches the Atlantic. The river's yearly flood cycle dictates the pace of life in this region. In the rainy season the river overflows its banks and spreads out until almost the entire valley is underwater. Villages, which are built on high ground, stand out as temporary islands. When the waters recede, crops are sown

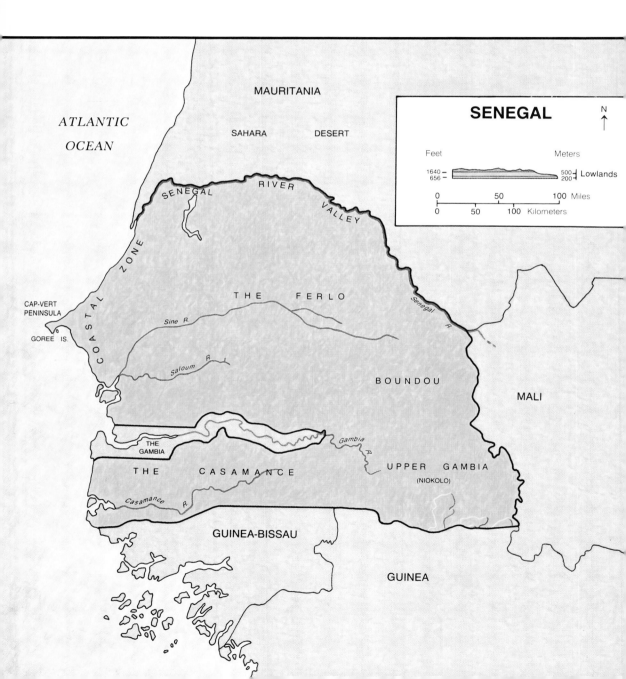

Photo by Hans-Olaf Pfannkuch

Basalt — a fine-grained volcanic rock — is strewn along the Senegalese shore near Yoff.

and harvested. Then, once again, the land becomes dry until the next seasonal flood.

The Ferlo is a broad plain that covers west central Senegal. The region receives only a small amount of yearly rainfall, which is absorbed very quickly into the porous, sandy soil. This soil and the lack of rainfall make agriculture difficult. Per-manent villages, therefore, are hard both to establish and to maintain in this area.

The eastern part of Senegal has two regional names. Its southern half is called Upper Gambia, or the Niokolo, and its northern section is known as the Boundou. Rainfall and other climatic conditions in the Boundou resemble those in the Ferlo.

Photo by Virginia M. Graham

In a village in the Ferlo region of west central Senegal, two men clear a piece of land using the slash-and-burn technique. This method requires that they cut down and set fire to the existing vegetation to make the plot usable for cultivation.

An aerial view of the Casamance River shows some of the many islets scattered throughout the waterway.

Farther south, in Upper Gambia, however, the rainfall increases and supports more abundant vegetation and animal life.

The Casamance—the southern region that is almost separated from Senegal by the Gambian republic—receives more rain than the rest of the country. Its humid climate and plentiful rainfall have created more varied vegetation. Consequently, the agricultural sector in the Casamance is more successful than it is in northern parts of Senegal.

Rivers

Three major rivers water large areas of Senegal. Although their sizes vary with the level of rainfall they receive, all of the rivers have navigable sections on their lower courses.

The Senegal River originates in the Fouta Djallon Mountains of Guinea and flows for approximately 1,000 miles northeastward into Mali. The river then turns westward into Senegal before eventually emptying into the Atlantic Ocean. As the river flows through Senegal, it acts as a dividing line between the Sahara Desert to the north and more habitable regions to the south. During the dry season, the Senegal's water level drops so dramatically that ocean tides travel as far as 300 miles upstream, creating saltwater swamps. During the rainy season, when the water level is high, the Senegal River is navigable by large vessels between Saint-Louis in northwestern Senegal and Kayes in Mali. Throughout the year, boats can travel upstream for only 175 miles, that is, as far as Podor, which serves as an important cargo port for nearby Mauritania.

The Gambia River also originates in Guinea, entering Senegal near the town of Kédougou in the southeast and flowing through the country for about 200 miles. The river's course then goes through the Gambian republic, where the river finishes its journey to the Atlantic Ocean.

The Casamance River is about 200 miles long and draws most of its water from the Casamance region. The river flows toward the Atlantic, forming an ocean estuary that is over five miles wide in some places. The region's most important seaport is Ziguinchor, which lies about 40 miles upstream.

Strictly speaking, the Saloum River—located just north of the Gambia—is not a river at all, since it would be dry for most of the year if the ocean did not fill its 100-mile riverbed with salt water. Thus,

while 60 miles of the Saloum are suitable for transportation, its salty waters are unfit for use in irrigation projects.

Climate

In most of the country, temperatures vary little between summer and winter. Seasons are distinguished primarily as either dry or rainy. Temperatures reach highs of 110° F during the day and drop as low as 60° F at night. Because Senegal lies in the tropics, periods of twilight are shorter

Irrigation and a hot climate have made it possible for Senegal to grow tropical plants such as pineapples *(right)* and papayas *(below)* in some areas.

than in the temperate zones. Thus, full daylight and complete darkness arrive quickly, rather than gradually.

The rainy season—between June and October—has an average annual rainfall of 10 inches in the north, 25 inches in Dakar, and 60 inches in the Casamance region. The dry season—from November to June —is virtually rainless. The rainy season begins in the south when the monsoon, a rain-bearing wind, reaches Senegal from the ocean and then pushes north across the land. The most frequent wind, called the harmattan, comes off the Sahara Desert and is hot and dusty. In contrast, during the dry months, an ocean current

Warthogs frequent the plains and open woodlands of central and northern Senegal. Their tusks are quite sharp and are used mainly to fight off predators, such as lions.

causes cooler temperatures in the coastal zone.

Fauna

Senegal supports a variety of animals, some of which live on a 430,000-acre game preserve in the southeast called Niokolo-Koba National Park. The largest concentration of animals—including lions, leopards, hippopotamuses, warthogs, gazelles and other antelope, savanna monkeys, and large Gambia rats—can be found at Niokolo-Koba. Poisonous snakes, such as pythons, vipers, cobras, and mambas, thrive in the Casamance region, and a small number of crocodiles are still found on the Senegal River and on the watercourses of Upper Gambia.

Among the most important and plentiful of the fish found off the coast of Senegal is the large Nile perch, or *capitaine*.

Lions are among the animals preserved in Niokolo-Koba National Park, where they are able to live and multiply in relative safety.

14

Leopards live in many parts of Africa, including Senegal, and often lie in wait for their prey to pass by.

Shores and estuaries are rich with shrimp and many kinds of saltwater fish. Farther out in the Atlantic, tuna, amberjacks, and dolphins are abundant.

Senegal has a particularly diverse bird population. Huge numbers of seabirds—pelicans, herons, egrets, cormorants, and various terns and ducks—inhabit the estuaries and the seashore. Among the land birds are ostriches, bustards, quails, partridges, and long-legged secretary birds. The forest is the home of hornbills and large groups of noisy parakeets. Vultures and kites are common near settled areas and are valuable as scavengers. Senegal also hosts migratory birds, which arrive each winter from the cold, northern climates of Europe.

Camels bite off the leaves of trees near Kaolack in central Senegal.

Flora

Because temperatures are fairly uniform throughout Senegal, the differences in vegetation from one region to another are caused by variations in rainfall and occasionally by soil conditions. Although the country is divided into several vegetation zones, it is frequently difficult to distinguish one zone from another in places where they overlap.

The Sahel, or savanna woodland, covers the northern part of the country (except for the coastal zone) and contains acacia trees, desert date trees, and small, thorny bushes. Most important of the many kinds of acacia trees are those used as cattle feed and as a source of gum arabic, which is used in making candies and medicines. With few exceptions, most of the plant life in this zone is native to the region.

The Sudan zone (not to be confused with the country named Sudan, located much farther east) covers the central part of Senegal. This area has a more varied mixture of grasslands and trees, many of which were introduced for food and commercial purposes. Trees found in this region are mahogany; the shea tree, which yields a vegetable fat called shea butter; and the *kinkeliba*, which has medicinal properties that can reduce fevers, such as those brought on by malaria.

Along the coast north of Dakar, a narrow belt of land—where rainfall is heavier and humidity is higher—is characterized by abundant vegetation. Oil palms, fruit trees, and garden vegetables are common. In areas nearer the ocean, however, the soil has a very high salt content and supports only vegetation that is resistant to salt, such as salt cedars, a few varieties of acacia and mimosa trees, and clumps of salt grass.

Because of the very heavy rainfall and well-soaked soil, the western part of the Casamance is the most heavily forested section of the country. Coastal channels and estuaries are bordered with mangrove thickets and groves of raffia and rattan

Independent Picture Service

Palm trees are plentiful in Senegal's warm climate. Gourds have been attached to these trees to collect their sap, which will be fermented into palm wine.

Courtesy of Tom O'Toole

In Senegal, huge trees are often encircled with long, twisting vines.

16

palms. Oil palms, mahogany, and teak grow on higher ground. Large areas have been cleared of trees and converted into rice paddies in this part of Senegal.

One of the most important trees in Senegal, as well as throughout Africa, is the baobab. Although its wood is too soft and spongy to be used as timber, its fruit is cooked and eaten as a vegetable, and the leaves are used in soups. Furthermore, the bark of the tree can be peeled off and made into rope or boiled down and used as medicine. People have been known to store water in the large, natural cavities of the trunk of the baobab.

Dakar

With a population of over 800,000, Dakar not only is the capital and principal city

Independent Picture Service

Among the most prominent landmarks in Dakar is the tiled minaret, or tower, of the Great Mosque.

Independent Picture Service

The baobab—a common tree throughout Africa—spreads its clawlike branches to the sky.

17

of Senegal but also is one of the leading seaports in all of Africa. In addition, until Senegal achieved independence in 1960, Dakar was the administrative hub of French West Africa, the colonial federation formed by France of its western territories. The city is a successful blending of new and old styles of architecture. Churches and mosques dot the cityscape, but perhaps the Great Mosque is the most impressive, with its high minaret, or tower, and beautifully tiled interior. Tall office and apartment buildings line the wide avenues, and magnificent administrative structures that remain from French colonial days house the independent government of Senegal.

Despite these signs of external influences, the Medina section is a clear reminder that Dakar is an African city. The Medina—a colorful quarter of the capital—houses more than 300,000 people in a jumble of old buildings, alleys, and narrow streets. The area is crowded with people who come from West Africa and beyond, and the streets are filled with the sounds of many languages. The huge market in

Markets in Dakar display homegrown produce, such as the vegetables offered by this vividly dressed vendor.

A fort off the coast of the island of Gorée once protected the area from unwanted visitors.

the Medina is crammed with every product imaginable—foods and spices from the interior, transistor radios from Japan, and raw honey from the Casamance. Flowers, vegetables, and woven goods ranging from vivid cotton prints to luxurious gold-threaded fabrics attract eager buyers.

Dakar—one of the most important seaports on the coast of West Africa—is large enough to accommodate 40 to 50 oceangoing vessels at one time. Besides being able to handle ordinary cargo, Dakar is also well equipped to provide water, food, and repair services for ships. Refrigerated warehouses and pipelines for oil and liquid chemicals add to Dakar's importance as a port.

The island of Gorée lies a little over a mile away from Dakar and was once well known as a slave-trading station. Africans

Dakar's urban development can be traced partially to its former position as capital of the Federation of French West Africa.

Dozens of ships at a time can be accommodated at Dakar's port facilities, which offer vessels a variety of repair and storage services.

were brought from the interior to the coast by black slave dealers. The captured humans then were taken from the mainland to Gorée in small boats and sold to European merchants, who took their captives to the New World.

Secondary Cities

Kaolack, with 136,000 people, is the leading town in the richest peanut-growing area in the country. In the last 70 years—as the value of the peanut crop has increased—Kaolack has changed from a small village into a city second only to Dakar in size and importance. A port for vessels that reach it via the Saloum River, Kaolack is at the end of a branch of the Dakar-Niger Railway and is connected with the Casamance district by a modern highway that cuts across the Gambian republic.

Located east of Dakar and with a population of about 114,000, Thiès is a major industrial, commercial, and communications city. Lying at the junction of main highways from Dakar to eastern Senegal, Thiès is an important market for peanuts and other crops grown in the region.

With a population of 100,000, Rufisque is an industrial town that has grown so much it resembles a suburb of nearby Dakar. Rufisque supports peanut-oil refineries, a pharmaceutical plant, and textile and shoe factories.

Situated at the mouth of the Senegal River, Saint-Louis (population 88,000) was once the capital, as well as the most important seaport, of the country. After the railway line between Dakar and Saint-Louis was completed, however, the city lost its place as a major commercial hub.

Women of the Wolof—Senegal's largest ethnic group—sort peanuts at Kaolack, the nation's main peanut-growing region.

Independent Picture Service

Nevertheless it remains the end point for Senegal River traffic and is the gateway to Mauritania, whose border lies just north of the city.

Founded by the Portuguese in 1645, Ziguinchor is the main city of the Casamance region and the commercial seaport for the farms, fisheries, sawmills, and peanut-oil complexes in the south. With a population of more than 70,000, it is one of the country's fastest-growing cities and has regular air service to Dakar, as well as to Conakry in Guinea.

Photo by Hans-Olaf Pfannkuch

A truck loaded with tons of peanuts leaves Ziguinchor in the Casamance for other commercial distribution points throughout Senegal.

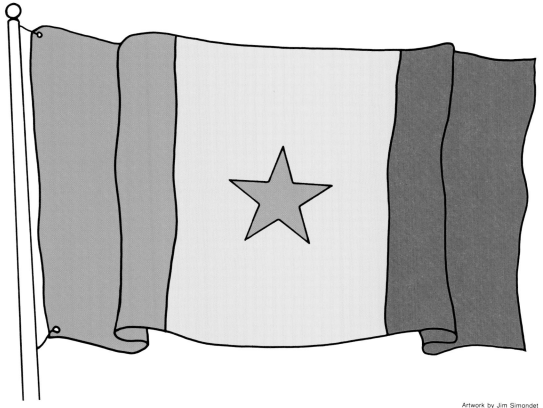

Artwork by Jim Simondet

The Senegalese flag is derived from the design used to represent the Mali Federation, of which Senegal was once a member. A green, five-pointed star–the symbol of African freedom–replaced the Mali emblem after Senegal declared its independence in 1960.

2) History and Government

Numerous stone monuments and burial sites testify to the long presence of humans in Senegal. Farming and fishing peoples lived in the area for thousands of years. Archaeologists have found wall paintings, tools, and pottery in the Senegal River Valley, and these remains suggest that a large-scale village—or even a city—existed at least 1,500 years ago.

The first written sources that mention the region are chronicles in the Arabic language. These records were kept by Arab traders who came across the Sahara from North Africa in the tenth century. The chronicles seem to indicate that the ancestors of modern Pular-speaking, Serer, and Wolof populations emigrated from lands to the north and east into the Senegal River Valley and other parts of the country.

From the tenth century, the people of Senegal had constant contact with North

Africa. Trading caravans came regularly to exchange goods and, periodically, to conquer and convert the local populations to the Islamic religion. In the eleventh century, Pular-speakers in the Senegal River Valley became the first large population to convert to Islam, while other groups adopted the faith in small, isolated areas.

Early Empires

From the fifth to the sixteenth centuries several large and powerful empires existed within and to the east of the area presently known as Senegal. These early empires were built around the trade caravans, with their valuable cargo of slaves, gold, salt, and spices that came and went through the Sahara Desert. In order to control and safeguard these caravans, strong armies were created, and the states that equipped the armies gradually extended their influence over larger and larger areas.

The earliest of these strong states, the Ghana Empire, flourished from the fifth to the thirteenth centuries. At its peak in the eleventh century, the Ghana Empire stretched from the Senegal River to Tombouctou, reaching deep into the interior of what is now Mali.

In the eleventh century, the Almoravids, desert-based Muslims (followers of Islam), conquered the Ghana Empire. They ruled for only about 15 years before the Ghana forces expelled them. Nevertheless, the invasion of the Almoravids seriously disrupted Ghana's trade—the lifeline of the empire. In time, the Ghana Empire began to decline, gradually giving way to the empire of Mali. Reaching its peak in the early part of the fourteenth century, the Mali Empire controlled an enormous area that included what is today the eastern part of Senegal.

By the end of the fourteenth century independent Senegalese realms began to develop along the empire's far north-

Photo by Virginia M. Graham

Senegal's early history is tied to Islam, the religion to which migrating Arab traders—who came to the area from North Africa—belonged. This pastel-colored mosque is in Touba, the holy city of the Murid sect of Islam.

23

An old engraving depicts a village of the Kru people—skillful boat handlers who were valued by early explorers and slave traders.

western fringes. Among these were the Wolof kingdoms, which were united by similar languages and cultures. For 200 years these monarchies dominated the coastal area from the mouth of the Senegal River to modern-day Thiès and as far as 150 miles into the interior. Pular-speakers continued to rule the middle Senegal River Valley, while Malinke peoples controlled the fertile areas of Upper Gambia and the Senegal River.

Arrival of the Europeans

In the fifteenth century the Portuguese, as well as other Europeans, wanted to overcome the trading monopolies that had been established between the eastern Mediterranean and the Orient. In search of alternate trade routes to Asia, Portuguese navigators set out to explore the Atlantic Ocean. They discovered the Madeira Islands, off the coast of Morocco, in 1418 and found the Cape Verde Islands and the

A Tukulor shoulders his musket after a day's work. The man's ancestors were among the first African groups to accept the religion of Islam.

Photo by Virginia M. Graham

Photo by Virginia M. Graham

After the decline of the Ghana and Mali empires, ethnic groups with similar traditions and ideas banded together. The ceilings of these two dwellings, both of which are made of wood and straw, suggest the similarities and differences of these peoples. The ceiling (above) of a Pular-speaker's house has a circular design, and the ceiling of a Wolof dwelling (left) is fashioned in squares.

25

The French settlement of Saint-Louis at the mouth of the Senegal River was thriving at the end of the eighteenth century.

mouth of the Senegal River in 1445. From these early outposts, the Portuguese established a profitable trade in slaves and gold all along the coast of Senegal.

Until about 1550 the Portuguese had exclusive rights to all trade along the West African coast. Gradually, however, merchants from Holland, France, and Great Britain began to undermine the Portuguese monopoly. By 1617 the Dutch had established settlements on the island of Gorée.

In the seventeenth century the French began to exert their influence along the Senegal River, sailing several hundred miles inland. In 1626 several French merchants formed a company for the commercial exploitation of the Senegal and Gambia rivers. The first French settlement—named Saint-Louis—was established in 1658 on an island at the mouth of the Senegal River. For the next 150 years, Saint-Louis was the base of all French activity and expansion in West Africa. In 1677 the French captured Gorée

from the Dutch and turned it into a naval base.

Within the area of Senegal and Gambia (sometimes called Senegambia), competition for control of trade pitted France and Great Britain against each other throughout the eighteenth century. The French had outposts at Saint-Louis and Gorée, while the British held the mouth of the Gambia River. Neither European power was able to eliminate the presence of the other, and this inability laid the groundwork for the establishment of a French colony in Senegal and a British colony in the Gambia. The long-disputed boundaries between the two colonies were finally agreed upon in 1889.

The Slave Trade

Although slavery existed within African societies before the arrival of European traders, the demand for slaves increased rapidly as the number of New World plantations multiplied. Senegambia provided one-third of the slaves captured and sold up to the beginning of the seventeenth century. After that time, the marketing of enslaved laborers decreased in Senegal, and other areas along the coast of the Gulf of Guinea became the main sources of supply.

Intense competition for slaves along the Senegal River in the late seventeenth century brought about a religious resistance movement that was led by Muslim leaders. This movement directed its assaults against the black, slave-trading aristocracy. The combined might of wealthy slave traders and of European firearms—supplied by the French at Saint-Louis—crushed the revolt.

French Colonization

At first the settlements in Senegal were considered little more than commercial bases, but, as France began to lose its colonies in the New World and Asia, Africa drew more French attention. In 1840 the French government decreed Senegal a permanent French possession and established

A slave cell at Gorée illustrates the crowded and grim conditions that greeted captured Africans, who were transported to the island to await sale and shipment to the New World.

Originally a Dutch outpost, Gorée was fortified to withstand attacks from other colonial powers. The French took over the island in 1677.

a new administration in Senegal with judicial and representative councils. Furthermore, the new administrators brought French-style education to Africans within the territory.

In 1848 the new French republican government, inspired by the struggles of its own people for freedom during the French Revolution, abolished slavery. Everyone born in the colony—black and white alike—was given full French citizenship. This new status enabled a few Senegalese (those who satisfied certain educational requirements) to elect a deputy to the French legislature in Paris. Four years later, however, a new regime came to power in France, led by Napoleon III, who revoked Senegal's right to be represented in Paris.

In 1854 General Louis-Léon-César Faidherbe was sent to control the frequent clashes among African kingdoms along the Senegal River. Toward this end, he created the *Tirailleurs Sénégalais* (Senegalese Riflemen), an army of local volun-

Independent Picture Service
Seku Ahmadu succeeded his father, al-Hajj 'Umar, as ruler of the Tukulor Empire in 1864. French advances into the interior decreased the king's military and political strength to a such a degree that by 1891 he was virtually powerless.

teers under French commanders who were later to achieve international fame as superb fighters. At the same time, Faidherbe began to lay the foundations that would make Senegal a prosperous and well-administered colony. An official newspaper, *Le Moniteur du Sénégal,* began publication in 1855, and the founding of the Bank of Senegal soon followed.

During much of the colonial period, Senegal and the Senegalese had advantages over later colonial possessions. The development of state schools made a European-style education available to Africans, and scholarships gave them the opportunity to continue their training in France, creating a French-educated, African elite.

The Late Nineteenth Century

Although trade between African groups and the French proceeded fairly peaceably, actual French occupation of African soil met with widespread resistance in Senegal.

Independent Picture Service
Louis-Léon-César Faidherbe served as governor of Senegal from 1854 to 1861 and from 1863 to 1865, during which time he extended and reorganized French territorial possessions in West Africa.

The architecture of the Hôtel de Ville (City Hall) in Dakar reflects the ornate, French-colonial style of the nineteenth century.

As the French penetrated farther into the Senegalese interior, they encountered the forces of the Tukulor Empire of Seku Ahmadu, who ruled from 1864 to 1893. In addition, the struggle of the Wolof kingdoms against French conquest lasted until the death of their leader Lat Jor in 1886. After the elimination of these two leaders, most of Senegal came under French control. In the Casamance, however, the Jola and other groups continued to fight the French into the twentieth century.

In the 1880s—partly as a consequence of the Berlin Conference, which sliced Africa into European spheres of influence —France decided to conquer more territories. The already established administration in Senegal served as a perfect base from which to start. In 1890 the French government embarked upon a plan to claim as much territory as possible.

By the turn of the twentieth century, the French flag had been planted across most of West Africa. French colonies also existed in North Africa and extended eastward and southward as far as the Congo. As late as 1895, Senegal included most of the territory of what are present-day Mali and Mauritania. Moreover, the French-appointed governor-general was given jurisdiction over all French West African territories, which had been combined into the Federation of French West Africa. In 1904 the French detached southern and eastern sections of Senegal to form French Sudan (modern Mali), and in 1920 the territory north of the Senegal River became Mauritania (independent since 1960).

Toward Independence

During World War II, the fall of France in 1940 led to the creation of a pro-Nazi government in Vichy, France, under Marshal Philippe Pétain. French officials and troops in Africa were faced with a difficult

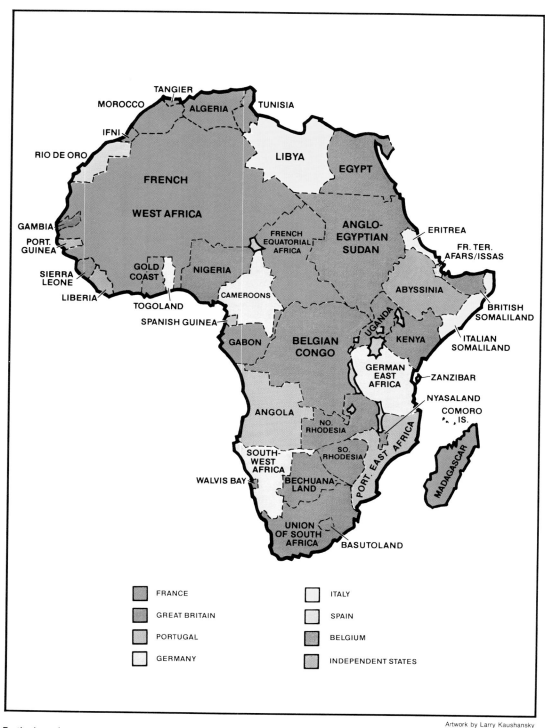

TANGIER
MOROCCO
ALGERIA
TUNISIA
IFNI
RIO DE ORO
LIBYA
EGYPT
FRENCH
WEST AFRICA
GAMBIA
PORT.
GUINEA
ANGLO-
EGYPTIAN
SUDAN
ERITREA
FR. TER.
AFARS/ISSAS
FRENCH
EQUATORIAL
AFRICA
SIERRA
LEONE
GOLD
COAST
NIGERIA
LIBERIA
TOGOLAND
CAMEROONS
ABYSSINIA
BRITISH
SOMALILAND
SPANISH GUINEA
UGANDA
KENYA
ITALIAN
SOMALILAND
GABON
BELGIAN
CONGO
GERMAN
EAST
AFRICA
ZANZIBAR
NYASALAND
COMORO
IS.
ANGOLA
NO.
RHODESIA
SOUTH-
WEST
AFRICA
SO.
RHODESIA
WALVIS BAY
BECHUANA-
LAND
PORT. EAST AFRICA
MADAGASCAR
UNION
OF SOUTH
AFRICA
BASUTOLAND

FRANCE
GREAT BRITAIN
PORTUGAL
GERMANY

ITALY
SPAIN
BELGIUM
INDEPENDENT STATES

Artwork by Larry Kaushansky

By the late nineteenth century, European powers had carved the continent of Africa into areas of influence. Present-day Senegal was included in the region called French West Africa. Map information taken from *The Anchor Atlas of World History,* 1978.

30

decision. The choice was whether to be loyal to the Vichy government in France or to the French forces in exile under General Charles de Gaulle. The governor-general of French West Africa and all the governors under him declared their loyalty to Pétain and the Vichy government. Many Senegalese, however, chose to support Free France and de Gaulle.

Because of the colonial support Africans had given to Free France, France had to revise its colonial African policies after World War II. French and African politicians put forth various proposals. Liberals wanted the full rights of French citizenship, while conservatives wanted to extend only those rights that the Senegalese already held to the rest of the French African colonists.

In 1946 liberals and conservatives reached a compromise that gave the colonies a new status by granting them membership in the newly created French Union. The agreement guaranteed the African peoples more representation in Paris and a greater voice in determining their own future. Between 1950 and 1958, further administrative rights were granted to Senegal, and complete independence became inevitable.

Since the early twentieth century, African political groups in Senegal had organized to participate in the direction of the region's affairs. The Senegalese Socialist party (PSS) wanted to legalize the founding of trade unions. A young PSS member named Léopold Sédar Senghor broke away and formed the Senegalese Democratic Bloc (BDS) in 1948. Among its social concerns, the new party urged the French government to increase funds to Senegal for education and health facilities. After it merged with the socialists in 1958, the BDS was renamed the Senegalese Progressive Union (UPS) and has called itself the Socialist party (PS) since 1976.

In 1964 Senegalese veterans of World War II took part in ceremonies celebrating the fourth anniversary of their country's independence.

Independence Achieved

In 1959, after long negotiations, Senegal and French Sudan decided to merge, forming the independent Mali Federation. Reluctantly, France agreed to accept this arrangement, but, partly because of rivalries and disagreements between the Senegalese and the Sudanese, the new federation was not a success. The Mali Federation was dissolved by Senegal, which declared itself an independent republic in 1960. Former French Sudan retained the name Mali for itself.

Léopold Senghor, who had emerged as a pivotal figure in Senegalese politics in the 1950s, became president of the newly independent Republic of Senegal. Instead of trying to confront opposition movements within his country, Senghor at-

Independent Picture Service

In 1966 Léopold Sédar Senghor *(right)* received an honorary degree, Doctor of Humane Letters, from Howard University in Washington, D.C. This recognition was as much a testament to the president's literary skill as it was to his role as the leader of a democratic African nation.

UPI/Bettman Newsphotos

Active in African politics since the late 1940s, Léopold Sédar Senghor became a spokesperson for socialist causes throughout the world. Here, he fields questions from reporters at a Socialist party congress in Lisbon, Portugal, in 1979.

tempted to absorb them into his own party. Opposition parties still exist in Senegal, and some hold seats in the legislature, but efforts to establish a strong second party have failed. A relatively free press, fairly active trade unions, and politically aware university students also help to assure that the government receives a constant influx of new ideas.

On December 31, 1980—after 20 years in office—President Senghor voluntarily stepped down, and his prime minister Abdou Diouf succeeded him. In February 1983 Diouf was elected by a wide margin to be the second president of Senegal. At the same time, eight parties put up candidates for election to the legislature. Its members—although overwhelmingly supporters of the PS—represent a wide variety of political opinions.

Since independence, Senegal has maintained friendly relations with countries of both the East and West and has especially close relations with France. President Diouf advocates regional cooperation among the countries of West Africa and supports African unity in general. Senegal

The 120 members of Senegal's national assembly meet in this modern building in downtown Dakar.

Bright red uniforms distinguish the presidential guard, who patrol the official residence of the Senegalese chief executive.

continues, in theory, to agree with Léopold Senghor's idea of global unity, which is meant to be achieved in stages, beginning on local and regional levels. A step in this direction was the creation in February 1982 of the Senegambian Confederation, which aims to unify the Casamance area with the rest of Senegal. The confederation also hopes to make the Gambia River a more useful waterway for both countries.

Government

The Senegalese constitution was adopted in 1963 and gives broad powers to a president, who is chosen by voters and serves a five-year term. The legislature is a unicameral (one-house) body of 120 members, who are elected at the same time as the president. The supreme court is the highest court in an independent judicial branch, and its judges are appointed by the president. Senegal is divided into 10 administrative regions, each headed by a governor, who is appointed by and responsible to the president.

33

Photo by Hans-Olaf Pfannkuch

3) The People

In 1987 Senegal's population was approximately 7.1 million. Two-thirds of the people live in rural areas, and the remainder are concentrated in cities and towns. Population density is heaviest in the west and forms a wide belt running along the coast. People move to the cities at a steady pace, particularly during the dry season when the land cannot be cultivated. At that time some farmers come to the cities to earn money and return home to work on the land as soon as the rainy season approaches.

Like most African countries, Senegal is inhabited by a large number of ethnic groups. In contrast to many other coun-

Independent Picture Service

While bargaining with fishermen for their catch, a woman in Dakar chews on a limewood stick, which acts as a sort of toothbrush.

represent about 15 percent of the population of Senegal, were herders, and today they can be found throughout West Africa and as far east as the Sudan. In Senegal most Fulbé live in the northern part of the tries, however, the groups live peacefully with one another and experience only occasional cultural conflicts. The largest ethnic group is the Wolof, who constitute nearly 40 percent of the population. They are followed in descending concentrations by the Fulbé, Serer, Tukulor, Malinke, Jola, and Bassari. As many as 100,000 non-Africans—mostly French, Lebanese, and Syrians—also live in Senegal.

African Groups

The Wolof—known by that name as early as the fifteenth century—spread out from their original state of Djolof. They gradually dominated other groups, who were forced to pay taxes and to swear loyalty to the Wolof conquerors. Most Wolof are found in Senegal, with a few small communities in neighboring African countries and in France.

Pular-speaking groups are usually divided into two subdivisions: the Fulbé and the Tukulor. Historically, the Fulbé, who

Courtesy of United Nations

A member of the Bassari, an ethnic group of southeastern Senegal, performs a traditional dance at a celebration in Dakar.

A fisherman at Kayar, a village northeast of the capital, walks among the brightly painted boats (called pirogues) that are a trademark of the port.

country, toward the middle of the Senegal River Valley, and in the upper Casamance region.

The Tukulor, who compose about 10 percent of the population, are concentrated in the Senegal River Valley. They are proud of their language, customs, and Muslim religion and tend to resist Western attitudes and values more than the Wolof do.

Traditionally, the Serer, who make up about 18 percent of the population of Senegal, have worked as fishermen along the coast and as farmers inland in the Saloum and Thiès regions. Through the centuries, they have resisted Islam, although in recent years many of them have been converted to the faith. About 10 percent of the Serer are Christian in a national population that is less than 5 percent Christian.

The Malinke—who speak languages derived from those of the former Mali Empire—represent less than 10 percent of the total population of Senegal. They are widely distributed over many parts of West Africa, mainly in Guinea, Côte d'Ivoire, the Gambian republic, and Mali. Most of the Malinke are involved in agriculture in the upper Casamance region, in Tambacounda, and in southeastern areas of the country.

A number of relatively small ethnic groups are concentrated in the southern Casamance region and in eastern Senegal. These groups speak languages that are not closely related to either the Pular-Serer-Wolof group or the Malinke-language families and include the Bassari, Manjak, and Jola. Historically, these peoples resisted being included in larger kingdoms and

Photo by Virginia M. Graham

A Malinke woman of the Casamance region sells tie-dye and batik products at a streetside market.

Photo by Virginia M. Graham

The local leader, or chief, of the Pular village of Dialacouna organizes a work force to clear a piece of land for gardening.

Known as attentive livestock raisers, the Fulbé often bring fresh milk to general collection points, such as this one near Saint-Louis.

empires and, consequently, were preyed upon by slave hunters and other exploiters. They still tend to be suspicious of governmental authority and often prefer to live peacefully in their own communities.

Non-Africans

Non-Africans, who number as many as 100,000, live chiefly in urban areas and are mostly of French, Lebanese, and Syrian descent. During the colonial period, when Senegal was the administrative headquarters for all of French West Africa, large numbers of French people came to the area as administrators, merchants, and technicians. After the country became independent, many of these foreigners chose to remain in key administrative, commercial, and industrial positions. Most French firms with offices in Senegal employ French personnel to run their affairs.

Until independence, social contact between the French and the Africans was limited, and the French excluded the Senegalese from many political and cultural

A country restaurant, located about 30 miles from Dakar, caters to a French clientele.

activities. After independence, the situation changed considerably, and the French no longer dominate Senegalese politics. The French, however, still are a major force in Senegalese trade and financial undertakings, despite assertive African efforts to take a leading role in these areas.

The French encouraged the Lebanese and the Syrians to settle in Senegal during the colonial period. These Arab groups were to serve as go-betweens for the French and the Africans, accepting jobs that neither the French nor the Senegalese wanted to undertake. The Lebanese and the Syrians became an important link between rural farmers and urban merchants. As middlepeople, they purchased the produce of the villagers—offering them consumer goods in exchange—and resold the produce to merchants or wholesalers in town. Many Lebanese became successful in their commercial enterprises and now control a good part of the country's business. Nevertheless, they have little social contact with the Senegalese.

Until recently, Western-educated Africans found jobs in the government more attractive than those in commercial, service, and production enterprises, which tended to be monopolized by Syro-Lebanese communities. More and more individuals and cooperatives of African origin, however, have begun to challenge the role of the Arabs in commerce and in industry.

Languages and Education

Although French is the official language of Senegal, generally it is used only by an educated minority of Senegalese. Wolof is the most common form of communication, since it is spoken by about 75 percent of the population. The government stresses

Independent Picture Service

Children of both African and European ancestry study together at a school in a modern residential development near Dakar.

39

the importance of Wolof but has not openly endorsed it as an official language. In addition to Wolof, most ethnic groups also speak their own tongues.

Two government-run radio stations broadcast from Senegal in French and in the leading languages of the country—Wolof, Malinke, Serer, and Pular. Most of the programs are educational, with a small number devoted to entertainment. An international radio station in Dakar conducts about 85 percent of its programming in French and the rest in English and Portuguese. Radio fills a vital need in reaching all parts of the country, since the spoken word is especially important in a land where most people do not read or write.

Historically, Senegal has had a greater number of highly educated people—at least in urban areas—than the rest of French West Africa. Nevertheless, the overall literacy rate is low—about 10 percent—and much still needs to be done to educate the Senegalese in rural areas.

Photo by Hans-Olaf Pfannkuch

The front page of Dakar's main French-language newspaper, *Le Soleil,* announces the competition between two strong teams—*deux géants* (two giants)—for the Africa Cup soccer match.

Courtesy of Tom O'Toole

Students gather round their teacher at a Muslim school on the island of Gorée.

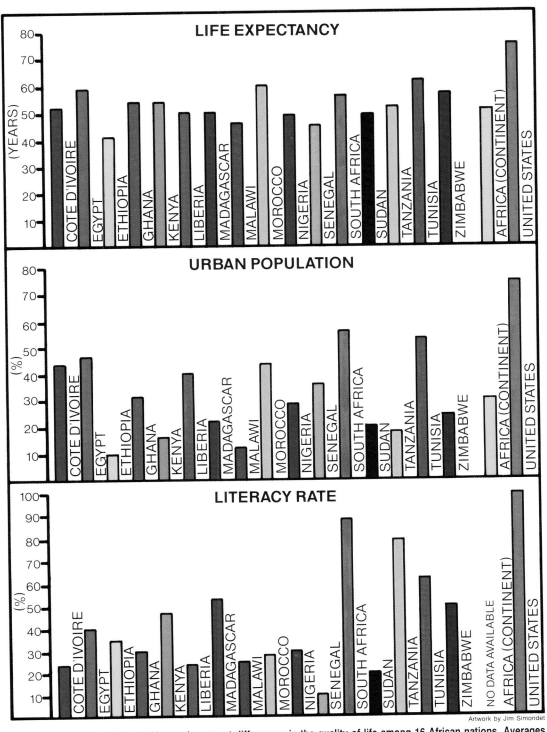

The three factors depicted in this graph suggest differences in the quality of life among 16 African nations. Averages for the United States and the entire continent of Africa are included for comparison. Data taken from "1987 World Population Data Sheet" and *PC-Globe*.

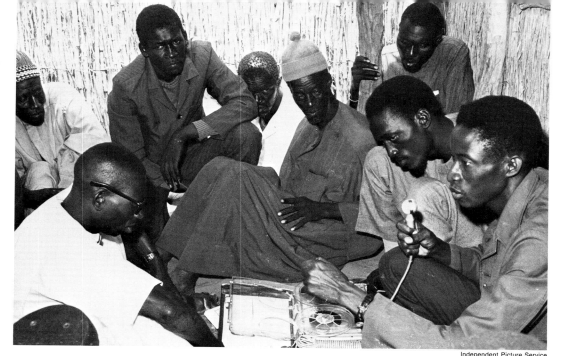

Interviewers from Dakar Radio prepare a rural educational program for farmers, who share their problems in front of the microphone and who, in return, receive professional advice.

Aware of the importance of education, parents are eager to send their children to school, when schools are available. Part of the problem, too, is that no single language is mutually understood. French— the language of Senegalese textbooks—is

In rural areas, where primary schooling has been inadequate, adults are given French language lessons.

42

To improve nutrition, schoolchildren receive cups of milk at their mid-morning break.

neither spoken nor comprehended by a majority of the student population. At present, 53 percent of school-aged children attend elementary classes. Eleven percent are enrolled in middle and secondary schools.

The University of Dakar has four major areas of study—literature, medicine, science, and law—and has a total enrollment of 11,000 students. Another 10,000 students attend vocational schools, which offer training in practical trades.

Health

Due to inadequate sanitation facilities, poverty, and poor nutrition, the country's level of health is substandard, except in Dakar and a few other large towns. The most evident sources of trouble are the insufficient and polluted water supply and the lack of proper sewage systems. Also harmful to the health of the Senegalese are anopheles mosquitoes, which transmit malaria and yellow fever, and the tsetse flies, which carry the virus that causes sleeping sickness.

Life expectancy is 45 years of age—a low figure when compared to the African average of 51 years of age. Infant mortality is higher in Senegal than in the rest of Africa.

In the mid-1980s an average of 131 infants died out of every 1,000 live births in Senegal. In comparison, the figure in Africa as a whole is estimated to be 113 deaths in each 1,000 live births.

The government is trying to correct unhealthful conditions, but the difficulties are discouraging. No hospitals or clinics exist outside the cities. Shortages of money and trained personnel make progress in attaining better health standards very slow. The government, with assistance from private French organizations and several United Nations agencies, has set up mobile hospitals and X-ray and laboratory units. These units travel from village to village, providing badly needed medical care and instructing people about hygiene and forms of preventive medicine.

Religion

About 90 percent of the people support the faith of Islam, the belief system based on the holy writings of the Koran as interpreted by the prophet Muhammad. A small number—including former president Léopold Senghor—are Christian; the remainder practice local religions.

Most Senegalese Muslims are members of local Islamic groups called brotherhoods. In Senegal two large groups of this kind exist—the Murid and the Tidjani. Their leaders wield considerable political power within the country because they can influence the way their members vote.

Many Senegalese continue to honor traditional beliefs and religious practices that are found throughout much of black Africa. Some Africans focus on a universal life force that they believe is everywhere in the natural order. Because they accept that such a life force can be concentrated in persons, animals, and objects, those who practice traditional beliefs seek to control this power for practical ends. For example, believers may hope to ensure a good harvest or to find a job. About 5 percent of Senegal's population supports this belief system, and most of the country's Muslim and Christian populations also accept some elements of these traditional ideas.

An elderly Muslim in Dialacouna fingers his prayer beads.

This member of the Murid brotherhood, a strong Islamic group throughout Senegal, lives in Dakar.

From the minarets at Touba, an Islamic holy city in the Ferlo, muezzins (Muslim criers) call the faithful to prayer.

The inner courtyard of Dakar's Great Mosque, where worshippers wash in the fountains before services, is intricately patterned with mosaic tiles.

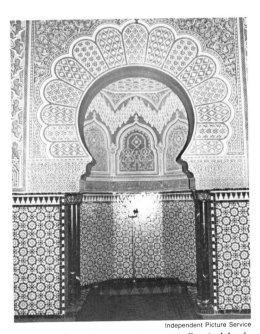

Inside the Great Mosque, where according to Islamic law neither furniture nor images are permitted, the floors are covered with fine carpets *(left)*. Elaborately tiled alcoves *(above)* are dedicated to the memories of particular religious teachers.

Photo by Hans-Olaf Pfannkuch

Using the speckled wings of butterflies, a Senegalese craftsperson has produced an image of a woman carrying a jar on her head.

Independent Picture Service

A basket maker fashions the bottom of a large container out of dried straw.

Independent Picture Service

The artist Younousse Seye uses seashells and thick oil paint to bring her ideas to life.

The Arts

Music and dance are the main forms of artistic expression in Senegal, with dancing the single most important creative outlet. In the past, ritual dances developed as part of religious or ethnic ceremonies. These elaborate traditional dances were adapted to serve the Islamic culture and have continued to exist, despite the arrival of European influences.

Senegalese dances are expressive, allowing a great deal of spontaneous movement

Photo by Hans-Olaf Pfannkuch

Carved wooden masks are still made throughout Senegal.

Using age-old techniques, two weavers produce vivid fabrics on handlooms.

within certain traditional forms. Emphasis is placed on group participation rather than on individual performance. Dances are usually accompanied by chanting and a few musical instruments, mostly drums and wooden xylophones, which in Senegal are called balaphons.

Until Muslim traders brought Arabic writing to Senegal, there was no written language. Consequently, only oral literature existed, mostly in the form of storytelling. The most famous storytellers in Senegal are the *griots*, who are not only entertainers but also play an important role in recording historical events. The griots also educate the young in the traditions of Senegalese society.

Since the 1930s, French-educated Senegalese writers have produced a significant number of novels, short stories, and essays. Written in French for Europeans and European-educated Africans, they deal almost exclusively with African themes. The most common subject is the attempt by Westernized Africans to reestablish their own cultural heritage and traditions alongside the powerful influences of Europe.

Before written languages existed, *griots*, or traditional storytellers, preserved the experiences of the Senegalese people. Here, a present-day griot begins a tale while watching the passersby on a village street.

Using a familiar rhythm, a woman shells peanuts, the main ingredient of peanut sauce.

Many of these works have been translated into English and have been published in the United States.

The Senegalese novelist and filmmaker Ousmane Sembene, for example, combines a distinctive writing style with strong political ideas. His major work, *God's Bits of Wood*, retraces the 1947–1948 strike of the workers on the Dakar-Bamako Railway. Among the country's other leading literary figures are the poets David Diop and former president Léopold Sédar Senghor, the novelists Abdoulaye Sadji and Mariamma Ba, and the historians Abdoulaye Ly and Cheikh Anta Diop.

Food

The Senegalese diet varies according to what foodstuffs are available locally. Along the coast and rivers, fish is a popular food item and is served in many differ-

ent forms. A favorite national dish is fish stew, made with several varieties of fresh fish, sea snails, dried fish, and vegetables seasoned with hot peppers. Tropical fruits, such as oranges, mangoes, bananas, and coconuts, are also available along the coast. Wherever irrigation is possible, okra, green peppers, tomatoes, and eggplants are grown in small gardens. For those living inland, the staple diet consists of starchy cereals like millet, sorghum, maize (corn), and rice. These items are pounded in large wooden bowls, then boiled to varying thicknesses and seasoned with different spices.

Because the typical Senegalese diet is high in starches and low in animal proteins and calcium, it is not always sufficiently nutritious. Milk and meat products are rare, except in large cities and among the Fulbé, who own herds of cattle. Meat is seldom eaten, except in the form of chicken or lamb stew.

While her little brother sneaks a nibble, a young girl cuts squash, which will be part of the family's main meal.

Photo by Virginia M. Graham

Tea is a popular beverage in Senegal, and this Serer man is brewing a pot spiced with sugar and mint.

Photo by Virginia M. Graham

Photo by Phil Porter

A field of peanuts—Senegal's most important agricultural crop—will take about four months to ripen. After harvesting, the plants may be used as feed for livestock.

4) The Economy

Although Senegal is more prosperous than some West African countries, it is still troubled by many economic problems. The nation's primary difficulty is that it has relied heavily on the raising of one crop— peanuts—for more than three decades. Inadequate farming methods, a low level of soil fertility, and periodic drought continue to plague Senegalese agriculture.

Agriculture

Peanuts make up about half of the total agricultural production and account for 30 to 50 percent of the country's export earnings. France is the chief buyer of Senegal's peanut crop, and for many years the former colonial power guaranteed a minimum price considerably above world figures. In 1968, however, France stopped the price subsidy, which meant that Senegal had to begin selling its peanut crop at competitive international rates.

Peanut growing was a state-run monopoly until 1985, yet only half of the revenue from peanut exports went to the growers. The other half was meant to be a financial safeguard against famine years, but the

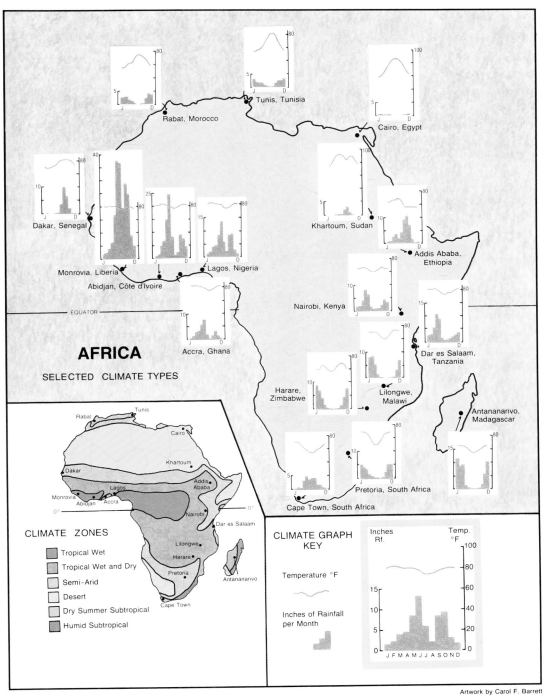

AFRICA

SELECTED CLIMATE TYPES

Rabat, Morocco

Tunis, Tunisia

Cairo, Egypt

Dakar, Senegal

Khartoum, Sudan

Addis Ababa, Ethiopia

Monrovia, Liberia

Abidjan, Côte d'Ivoire

Lagos, Nigeria

EQUATOR

Accra, Ghana

Nairobi, Kenya

Dar es Salaam, Tanzania

Harare, Zimbabwe

Lilongwe, Malawi

Antananarivo, Madagascar

Pretoria, South Africa

Cape Town, South Africa

CLIMATE ZONES

Rabat
Tunis
Cairo
Khartoum
Dakar
Addis Ababa
Lagos
Monrovia
Accra
Abidjan
Nairobi
Dar es Salaam
Lilongwe
Harare
Pretoria
Antananarivo
Cape Town

0°

- Tropical Wet
- Tropical Wet and Dry
- Semi-Arid
- Desert
- Dry Summer Subtropical
- Humid Subtropical

CLIMATE GRAPH KEY

Inches Rf.

Temp. °F

Temperature °F

Inches of Rainfall per Month

J F M A M J J A S O N D

Artwork by Carol F. Barrett

These climate graphs show the monthly change in the average rainfall received and in the average temperature from January to December for the capital cities of 16 African nations. On the graph for Dakar, Senegal, note that, although the capital is classified as having a semi-arid climate, the midsummer months receive substantial rainfall. North and east of Dakar, the climate becomes noticeably drier. Data taken from *World-Climates* by Willy Rudloff, Stuttgart, 1981.

A huge mound of harvested peanuts waits to be bagged, transported, and marketed.

money actually went to fund government projects or to support the administrative bureaucracy in Dakar. In 1985 President Diouf put an end to the government monopoly of the peanut market.

Other crops that are cultivated on a large scale are millet and sorghum. Cotton has proved to be a promising new cash crop, and the success of experimental plantings has encouraged cultivation on a larger scale. Crops grown on a smaller scale are sugarcane, maize, cassava (a fleshy, root crop), and beans. Senegal is not self-sufficient in foodstuffs, and a large amount of grain and other foods must be imported.

At Fatick in central Senegal, a worker operates a peanut-cleaning machine.

Small, low-cost farm equipment—such as a motorized, hand-guided tiller—has helped to modernize Senegal's agricultural production.

Wolof women sort red peppers that were cultivated in their village garden.

Photo by Hans-Olaf Pfannkuch

Members of a women's farming cooperative inspect the progress of their compost heap—a mound of natural fertilizers derived from decaying organic materials.

Photo by Hans-Olaf Pfannkuch

A woman who lives in the farming region between the Sine and Saloum rivers tends her field.

Photo by Hans-Olaf Pfannkuch

Although not self-sufficient in foodstuffs, Senegal is trying to broaden its agricultural production. Here, technicians inspect the irrigation works of a rice paddy.

In addition to peanuts, sorghum (a cereal grain) is also produced on a large scale. Bags of the crop are sewn shut at dockside before being shipped to Mauritania, a country that is suffering from severe drought.

Garden vegetables—such as watermelons, squash, okra, eggplants, tomatoes, and peppers—are cultivated along the coast in considerable quantities. Farther inland, however, these crops are planted on a very small scale, mostly for home consumption. The oil palm grows wild, and its nuts provide palm oil, which is a basic ingredient in African cooking.

Tobacco is grown in small quantities for home use, and tropical fruits—mangoes, coconuts, and citrus fruits—are raised along the coast, but not in large enough amounts for export. In more remote areas, many wild products, such as wild honey and the leaf and fruit of the baobab tree, supplement the Senegalese diet.

At Ziguinchor in the Casamance region, a worker collects gourds filled with palm tree sap, from which a fermented drink is made.

Cattle and goats graze in the parched land of west central Senegal. During years in which the country has experienced drought, many livestock have died for lack of water and pastureland.

Livestock raising is not a major factor in the economy of the country, despite the fairly large number of cattle, sheep, goats, horses, donkeys, and camels in Senegal. To many Fulbé, however, cattle raising represents a way of life, although the animals are considered more as symbols of dignity and personal status than as the means of financial gain. During the dry season and when droughts occur, the Fulbé travel great distances to supply their herds with water.

In the Sine-Saloum region a herdsman pumps up water to satisfy the thirst of his donkeys.

Bags of relief food from the World Health Organization arrive at the port of Dakar for transport to other areas of the drought-stricken Sahel, located just below the Sahara Desert.

The Great Drought

In the early 1970s Senegal began to experience a disastrous drought that also hit most other countries located in the Sahel just below the Sahara Desert. By 1973 the drought reached such alarming proportions that it is considered the worst on record in the region since ancient times.

The country's chief crop—peanuts—was heavily damaged, and livestock died in large numbers because pasturelands dried up. Many areas of Africa have been subject to occasional droughts, but United Nations experts suspect that this time human activities—such as overgrazing of animals and overcutting of trees—significantly changed the region's climate.

The United Nations conducted a large-scale relief effort to distribute foodstuffs donated by the United States, France, the Soviet Union, Canada, China, and the European Economic Community. Rainfall levels rose in 1985, which helped to ease the very serious conditions that resulted from the years of drought, but the agricultural sector in Senegal is only beginning to recover.

Fishing

With its long Atlantic coastline, Senegal recently has concentrated on expanding its fishing industry. The coastal waters are well-stocked with tuna, oysters, lobsters, and shrimp. Since the acquisition of modern fishing vessels, fishing has become a more important enterprise in Senegal. Foreign experts have assisted Senegal in developing modern, scientific fishing methods, and the industry now employs over 10,000 people. Much of the fish is canned for export and for shipment to more remote areas of the country. These processed food products help to provide rural people with sources of protein. In the mid-1980s export earnings of fish products rose by 47 percent.

Mining and Industry

Extraction of minerals has taken place largely in the more accessible western part of the country. Nevertheless, the eastern

Photo by Virginia M. Graham

A fisherman prepares to throw his net in a waterway near Dialacouna.

Photo by Hans-Olaf Pfannkuch

With improvements in commercial fishing methods, fish markets—such as this one at Mbour on Senegal's coast—have a larger catch to offer for sale.

58

Sacks of fertilizer are stacked by conveyor at a plant in Mbao.

region is being explored for valuable deposits of zinc, copper, and lead. The coastal zone has large quantities of titanium-filled sand, which yields zircon, a mineral used in gem making. Large rock deposits contain calcium phosphate, which is a valuable source of phosphate fertilizer. Limestone, used in cement manufacturing, is abundant in the Rufisque area. Petroleum deposits are known to exist off the coast of the Casamance region, and natural gas has been found near Dakar.

Although Senegal has more industry than most countries in West Africa, it cannot be considered an industrial country because its economy is basically agricultural. One of the most important sectors of the country's industry is peanut-oil processing, which alone accounts for about 25 percent of the total industrial output. Existing industries consist of cement- and shoe-manufacturing plants and some recently established textile mills. Other industries manufacture chemicals, paper, furniture, and electrical products.

A worker inspects bicycle tires produced by a company that received international financing from the World Bank.

59

Transportation

Over 2,000 miles of main roads and about 8,000 miles of secondary roads have been built in Senegal. The road system has not expanded much in the last 20 years, but the quality of existing thoroughfares is constantly being improved. Since most of the materials needed for modern highways are not available in Senegal, building techniques have been adapted to local conditions and supplies. Roads surfaced with seashells, sand, or soil mixed with oil and chemical stabilizers are not uncommon.

About 700 miles of railway connect Dakar with the rest of Senegal. At Thiès the railway branches out to Saint-Louis and to Bamako and Koulikoro in Mali. This line is called the Dakar-Niger Railway because it connects Dakar on the Atlantic coast to the Niger River in the interior. The French built the railways, which were designed to carry both freight and passenger traffic, during colonial days. The railway's purpose was to link the coast—with its well-developed ports—to Koulikoro on the Niger River. At Koulikoro the riverboats coming

Air Afrique, jointly owned by several West African countries, flies to Europe and North America, as well as throughout Africa.

Independent Picture Service

An all-weather highway connects Senegal's Dakar-Yoff International Airport with the capital.

Courtesy of John H. Peck

People in rural areas often travel from village to village in brightly painted vans, which are a familiar sight in West Africa.

from as far inland as Tombouctou and Gao in the Sahara Desert could unload their cargo for shipment to coastal markets.

By 1925 Dakar was linked with France via Casablanca, Morocco, for airmail service. By the mid-1930s regular passenger flights flew to Paris, and mail service was routed to South Africa and Brazil. In 1939 Air France began to provide domestic air service to Senegal and other destinations in French West Africa. Dakar-Yoff International Airport is now one of West Africa's major air links with the rest of the world.

After gaining their independence, 11 West African countries formed a jointly owned airline called Air Afrique. Each member-country owns 6 percent of the airline; the balance is owned by a private French airline and by the French government. Air Afrique is a vital link between countries of West and Central Africa and connects Dakar with Europe and the United States.

Despite roads, railways, and air traffic, traveling by foot is still common in Senegal.

61

A women's farming cooperative in the Casamance region cultivates oil palms, which yield an oil widely used in cooking African foods.

Dakar's port facilities are well known to international shippers, and the capital's already established industrial services may also help to put Senegal on a firmer financial footing.

A woman and her child lean on a piece of furniture whose covering is imprinted with the image of Senegal's president, Abdou Diouf, who was elected in 1983.

Photo by Virginia M. Graham

The Future

In the mid-1980s President Diouf enacted plans designed to stir activity in agriculture and industry. Serious efforts are necessary to broaden the scope of the nation's agricultural output and to release the economy from its heavy dependence on the peanut crop. The effects of the long drought of the 1970s and 1980s may be declining, and good facilities already exist for the development of industry.

Progress in improving the economy is slow, however, and the Senegalese are eager for a better and fairer distribution of the nation's income. A source of considerable national stability is the fact that Senegal's many ethnic groups—who form a human mosaic of the history of West Africa —have lived peacefully together for many years. This ability to co-exist may prove to be a decisive factor in Senegal's future growth and development.

Index